VOL. 75

LEONARD
GUITAR PLAY-ALONG

AUDIO ACCESS INCLUDED

PLAYBACK+
Pitch • Balance • Loop

Tom Petty

To access audio visit:
www.halleonard.com/mylibrary

5247-1374-7906-6917

Cover photo: Dennis Callahan

Tracking, mixing, and mastering by Jake Johnson & Bill Maynard at Paradyme Productions
All guitars by Doug Boduch
Bass by Tom McGirr
Keyboards by Warren Wiegratz
Drums by Scott Schroedl

ISBN 978-1-4234-1848-1

Visit Hal Leonard Online at
www.halleonard.com

HAL•LEONARD®
7777 W. BLUEMOUND RD. P.O. BOX 13819
MILWAUKEE, WISCONSIN 53213

Guitar Notation Legend

THE MUSICAL STAFF shows pitches and rhythms and is divided by bar lines into measures. Pitches are named after the first seven letters of the alphabet.

TABLATURE graphically represents the guitar fingerboard. Each horizontal line represents a string, and each number represents a fret.

4th string, 2nd fret   1st & 2nd strings open, played together   open D chord

HALF-STEP BEND: Strike the note and bend up 1/2 step.

WHOLE-STEP BEND: Strike the note and bend up one step.

GRACE NOTE BEND: Strike the note and bend up as indicated. The first note does not take up any time.

SLIGHT (MICROTONE) BEND: Strike the note and bend up 1/4 step.

BEND AND RELEASE: Strike the note and bend up as indicated, then release back to the original note. Only the first note is struck.

PRE-BEND: Bend the note as indicated, then strike it.

VIBRATO: The string is vibrated by rapidly bending and releasing the note with the fretting hand.

PALM MUTING: The note is partially muted by the pick hand lightly touching the string(s) just before the bridge.

HAMMER-ON: Strike the first (lower) note with one finger, then sound the higher note (on the same string) with another finger by fretting it without picking.

PULL-OFF: Place both fingers on the notes to be sounded. Strike the first note and without picking, pull the finger off to sound the second (lower) note.

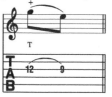

LEGATO SLIDE: Strike the first note and then slide the same fret-hand finger up or down to the second note. The second note is not struck.

SHIFT SLIDE: Same as legato slide, except the second note is struck.

PINCH HARMONIC: The note is fretted normally and a harmonic is produced by adding the edge of the thumb or the tip of the index finger of the pick hand to the normal pick attack.

TRILL: Very rapidly alternate between the notes indicated by continuously hammering on and pulling off.

TAPPING: Hammer ("tap") the fret indicated with the pick-hand index or middle finger and pull off to the note fretted by the fret hand.

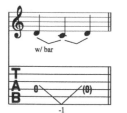

NATURAL HARMONIC: Strike the note while the fret-hand lightly touches the string directly over the fret indicated.

TREMOLO PICKING: The note is picked as rapidly and continuously as possible.

VIBRATO BAR DIVE AND RETURN: The pitch of the note or chord is dropped a specified number of steps (in rhythm) then returned to the original pitch.

VIBRATO BAR SCOOP: Depress the bar just before striking the note, then quickly release the bar.

VIBRATO BAR DIP: Strike the note and then immediately drop a specified number of steps, then release back to the original pitch.

Additional Musical Definitions

> (accent)	• Accentuate note (play it louder)	**Fill** — • Label used to identify a brief melodic figure which is to be inserted into the arrangement.
. (staccato)	• Play the note short	**N.C.** — • No Chord
D.S. al Coda	• Go back to the sign (𝄋), then play until the measure marked *"To Coda,"* then skip to the section labelled *"Coda."*	• Repeat measures between signs.
D.C. al Fine	• Go back to the beginning of the song and play until the measure marked *"Fine"* (end).	**1. 2.** — • When a repeated section has different endings, play the first ending only the first time and the second ending only the second time.

HAL•LEONARD®

GUITAR
PLAY-ALONG

AUDIO
ACCESS
INCLUDED

VOL. 75

Tom Petty

CONTENTS

American Girl

Words and Music by Tom Petty

Intro
Moderate Rock ♩ = 118

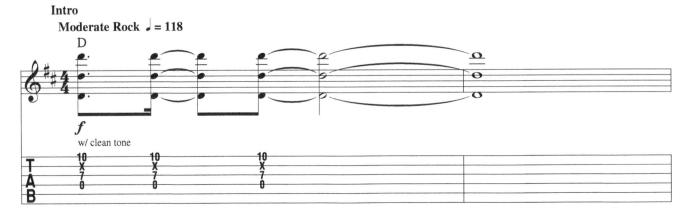

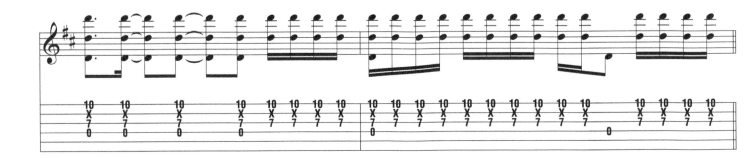

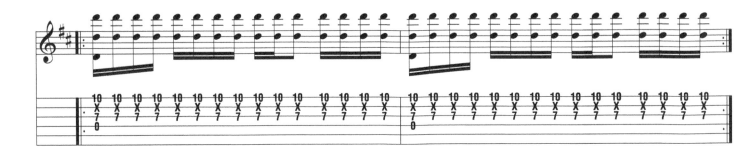

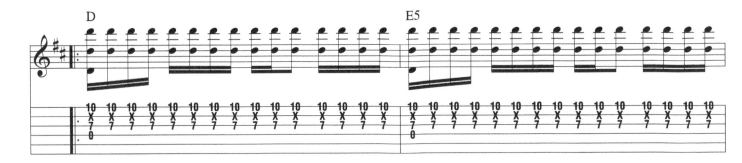

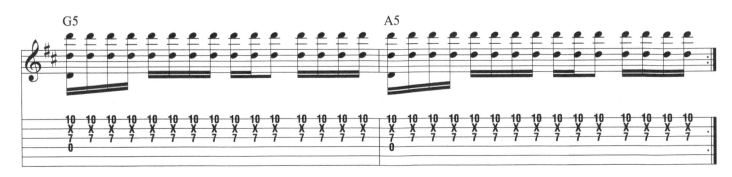

Verse

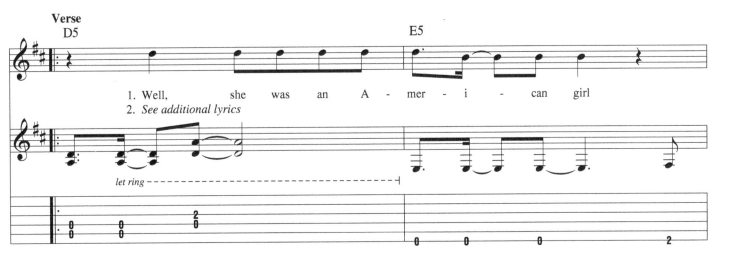

1. Well, she was an A - mer - i - can girl
2. *See additional lyrics*

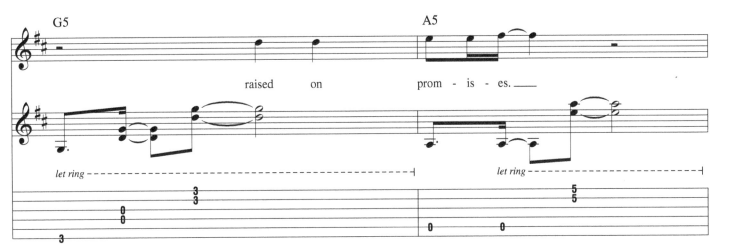

raised on prom - is - es. ___

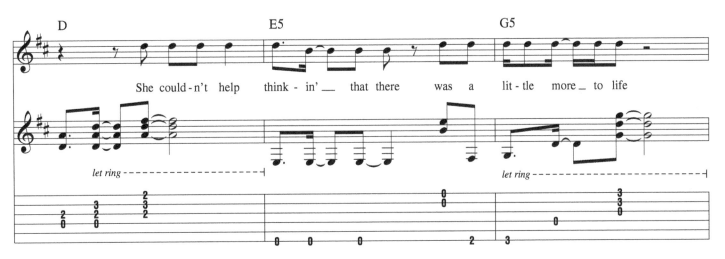

She could-n't help think - in' ___ that there was a lit - tle more ___ to life

some - where ___ else. ___ Af - ter all it was a great big ___ world ___

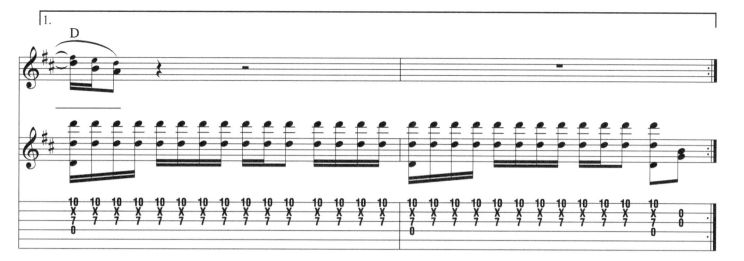

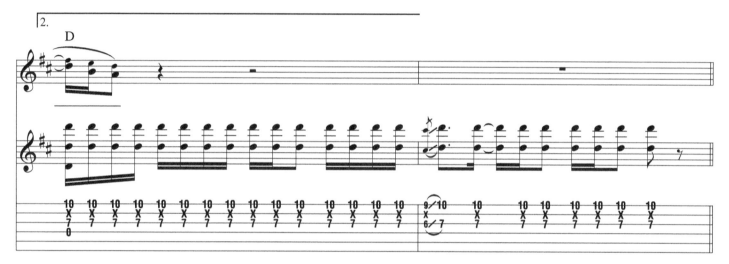

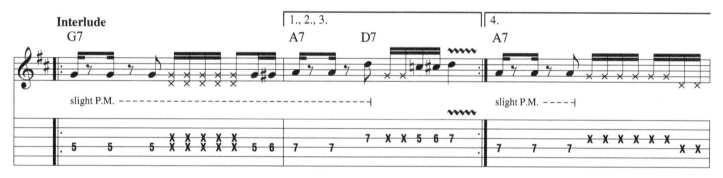

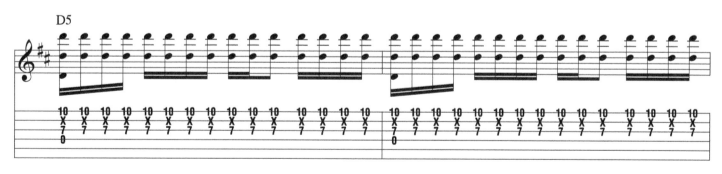

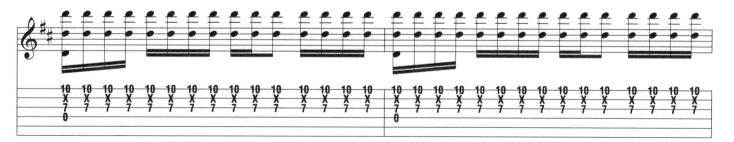

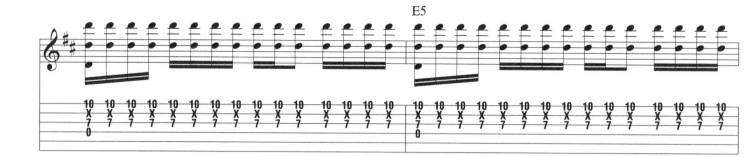

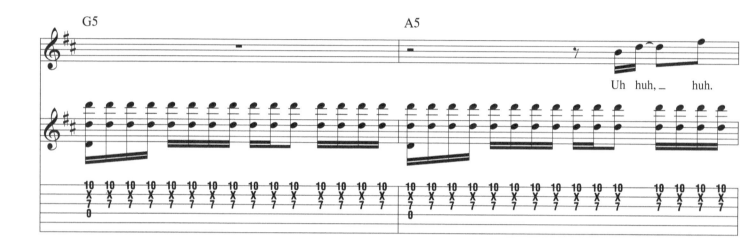

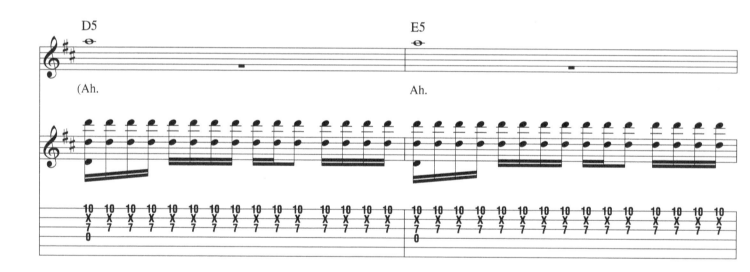

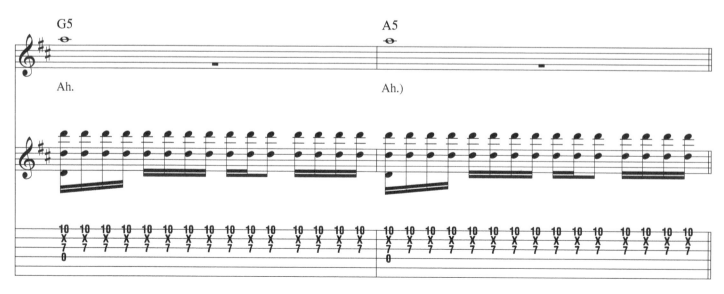

Outro-Guitar Solo

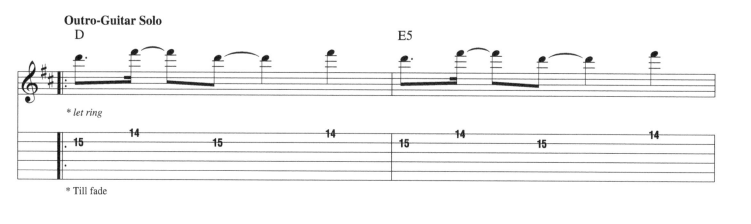

* let ring

* Till fade

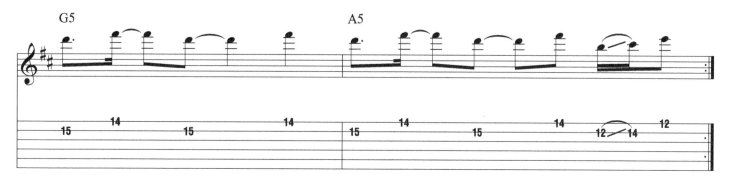

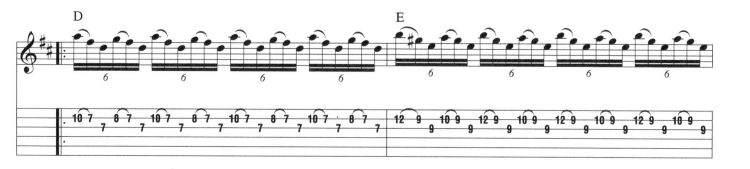

Repeat and fade

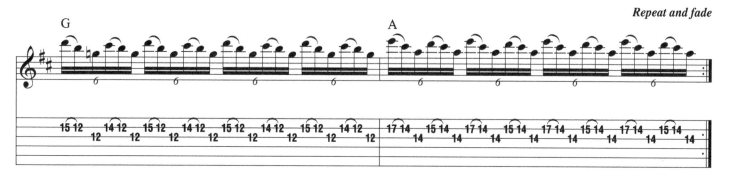

Additional Lyrics

2. Well, it was kind a cold that night.
   She stood all alone over the balcony.
   Yeah, she could hear the cars roll by out on 441
   Like waves crashin' on the beach.
   And for one desperate moment there,
   He crept back in her memory.
   God, it's so painful when somethin' that is so close
   Is still so far out of reach.

I Won't Back Down

Words and Music by Tom Petty and Jeff Lynne

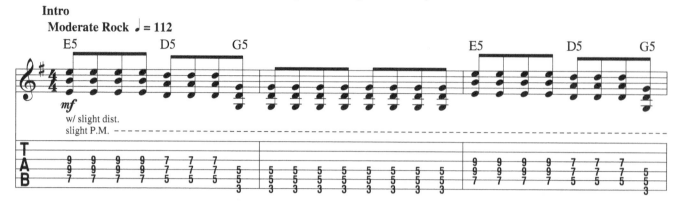

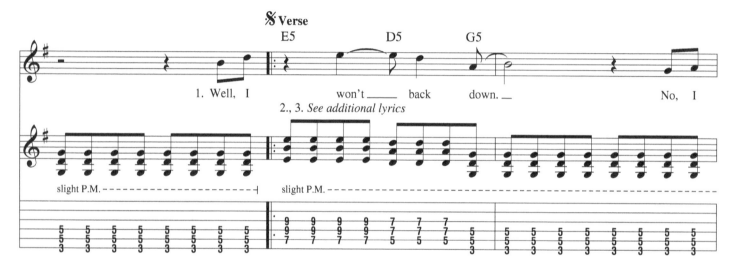

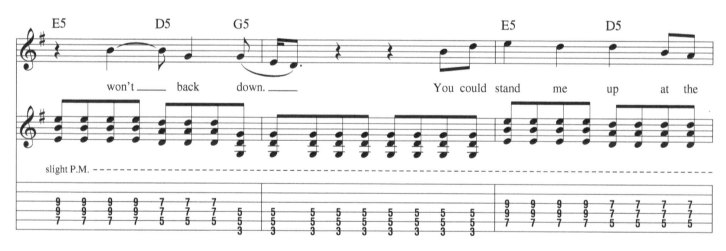

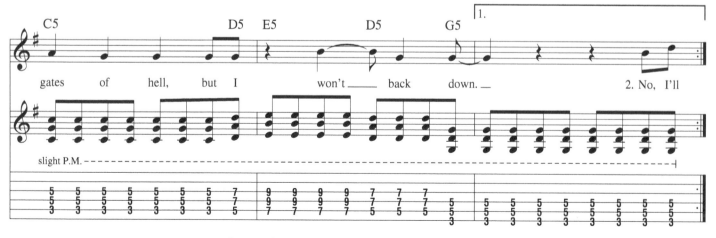

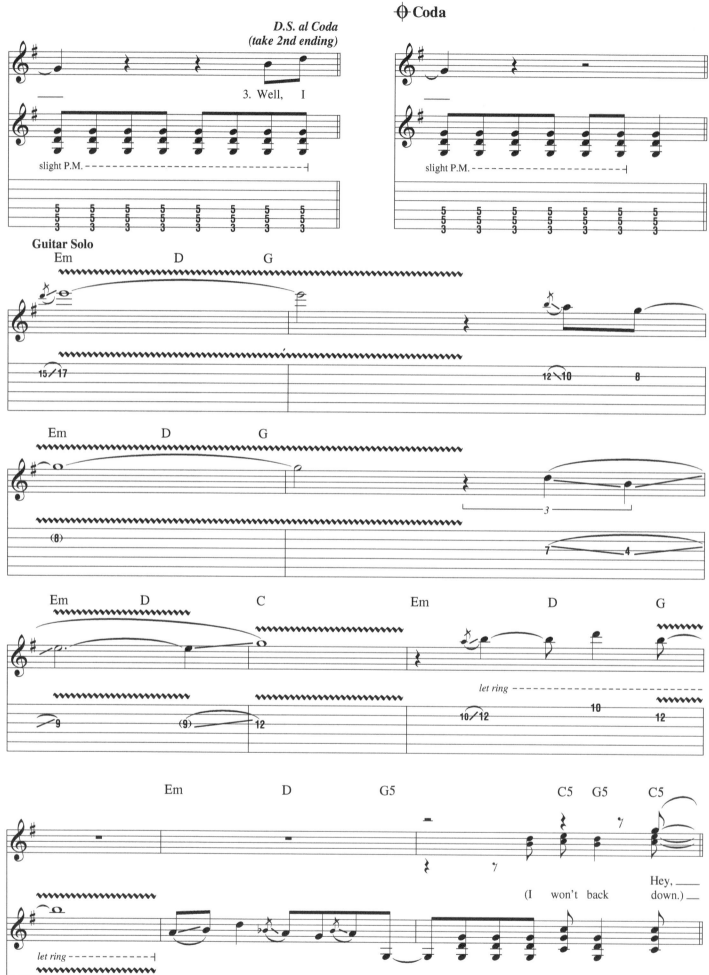

Chorus

ba - by, there ain't no eas - y way out.

slight P.M.

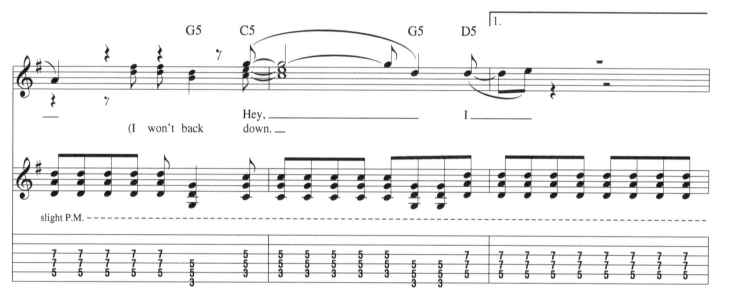

(I won't back down. Hey, I

slight P.M.

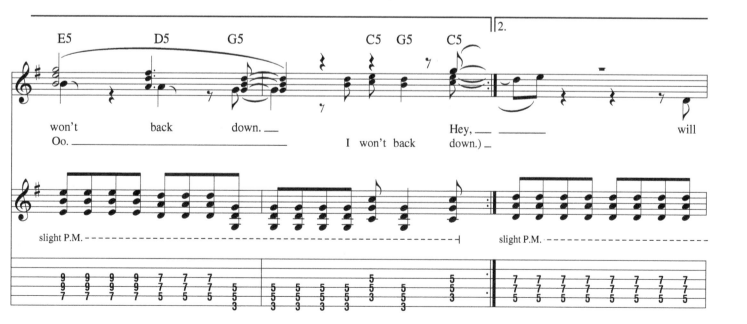

won't back down. Oo. I won't back down.) Hey, will

slight P.M.

slight P.M.

13

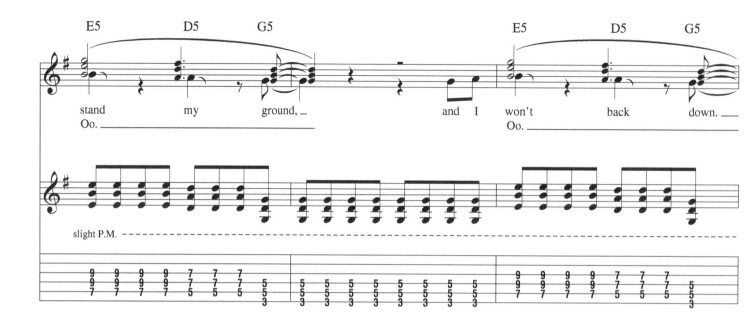

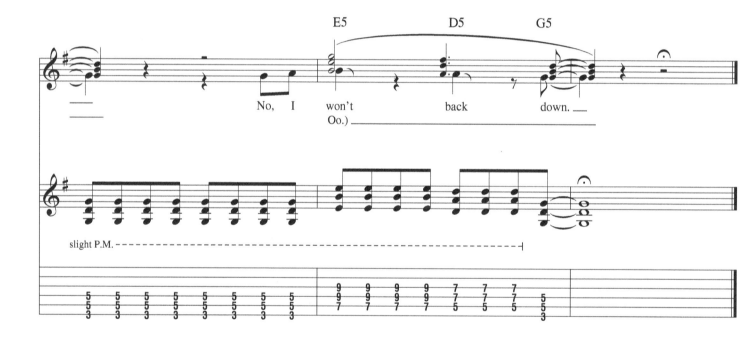

Additional Lyrics

2. No, I'll stand my ground.
Won't be turned around.
And I'll keep this world from draggin' me down,
Gonna stand my ground.
And I won't back down.

3. Well, I know what's right.
I got just one life
In a world that keeps on pushin' me around.
But I'll stand my ground,
And I won't back down.

Runnin' Down a Dream

Words and Music by Tom Petty, Jeff Lynne and Mike Campbell

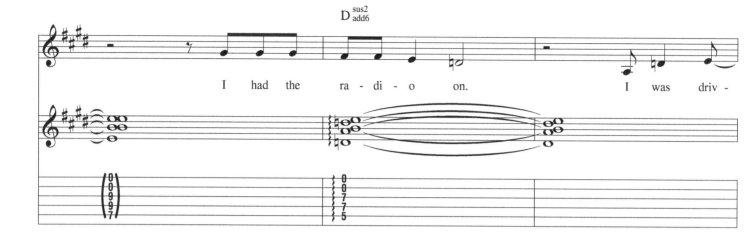

D_{add6}^{sus2}

I had the ra - di - o on.
I was driv-

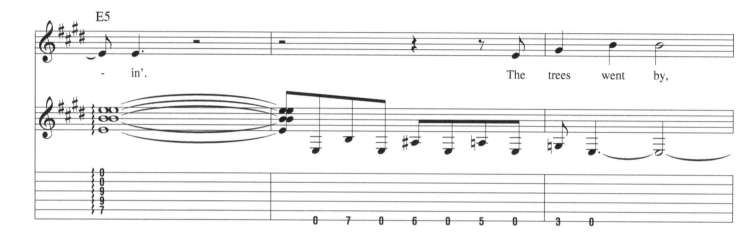

E5

- in'.
The trees went by,

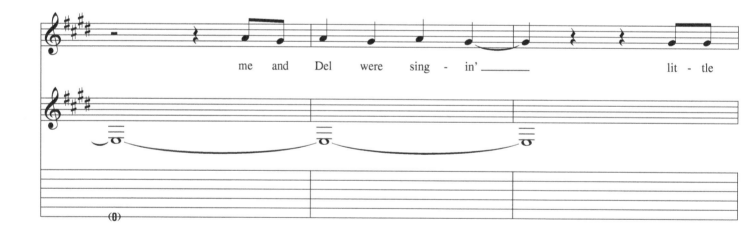

me and Del were sing - in'
lit - tle

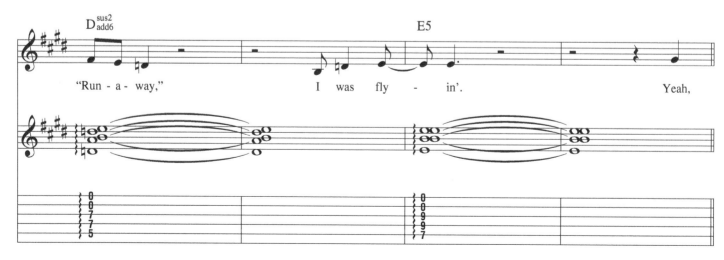

D_{add6}^{sus2}
E5

"Run - a - way,"
I was fly - in'.
Yeah,

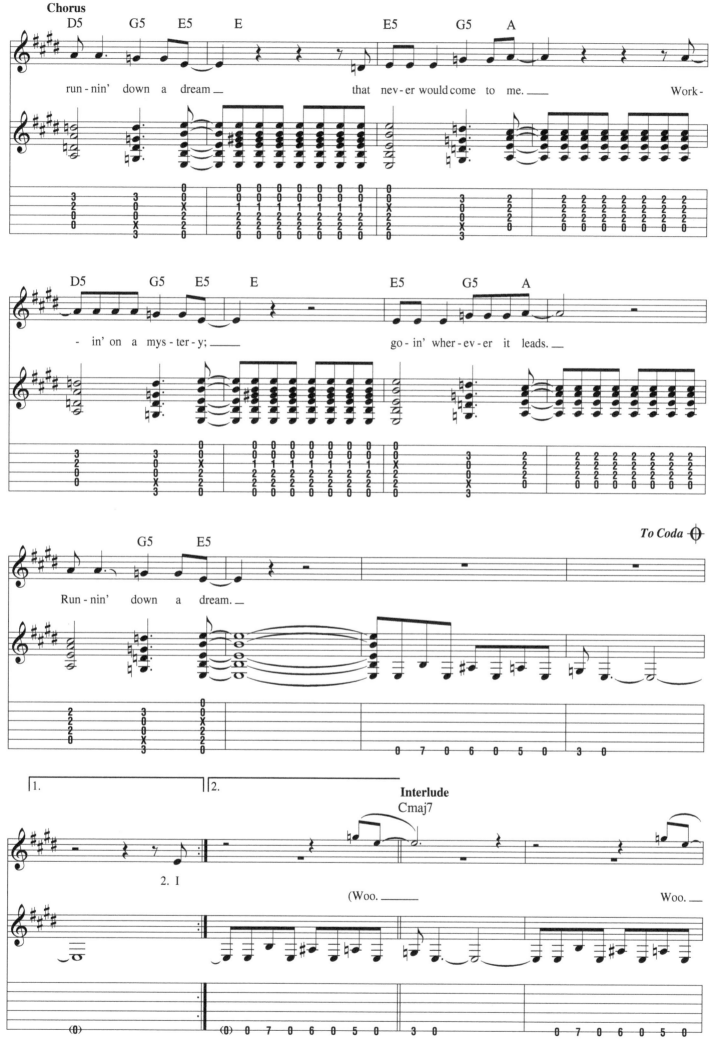

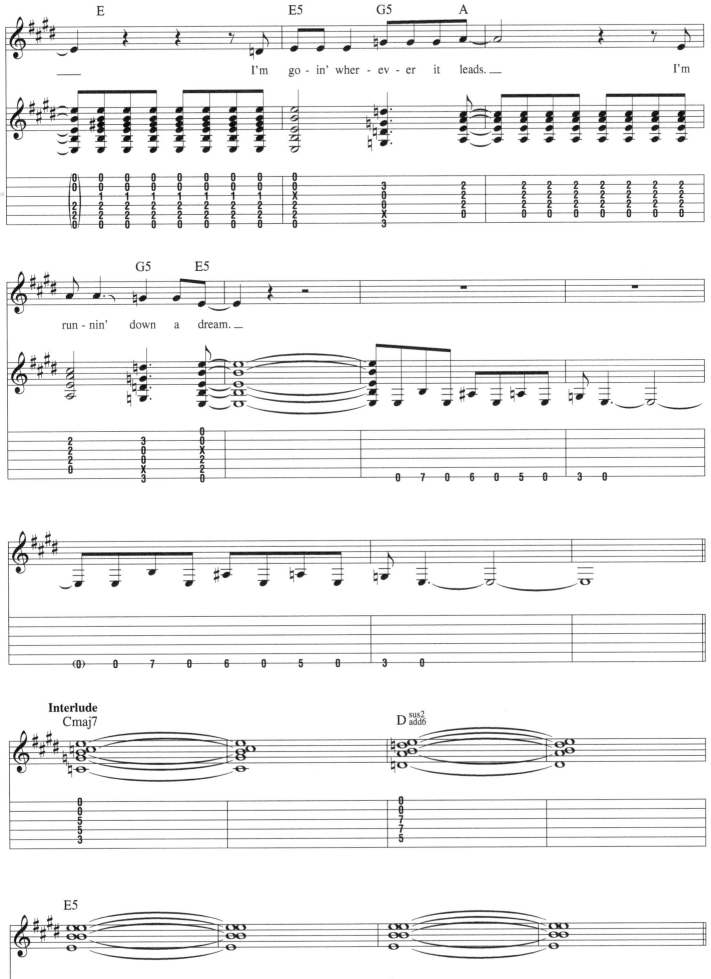

Outro-Guitar-Solo

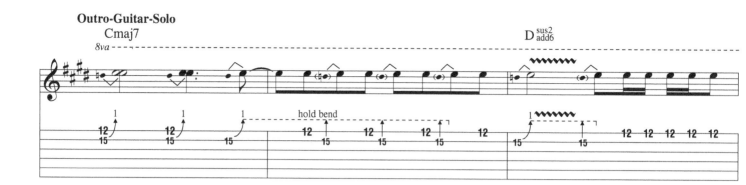

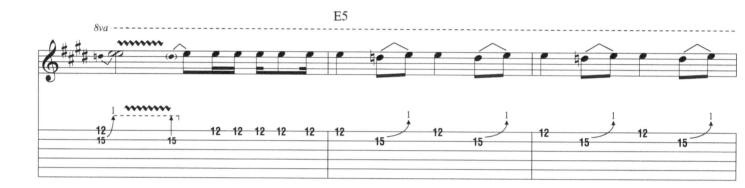

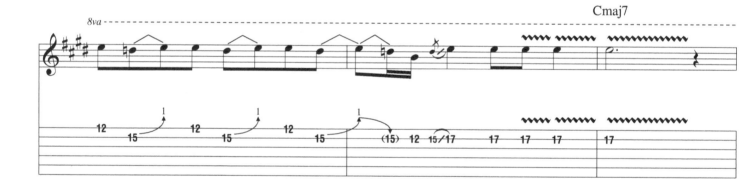

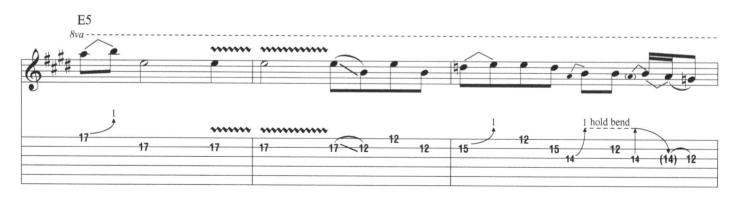

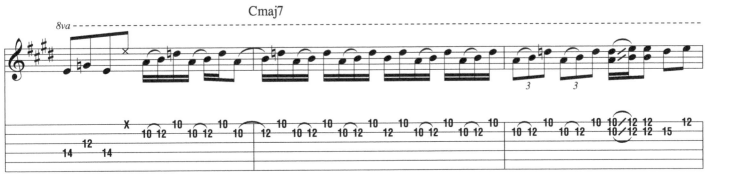

Cmaj7

D$_{add6}^{sus2}$ E5

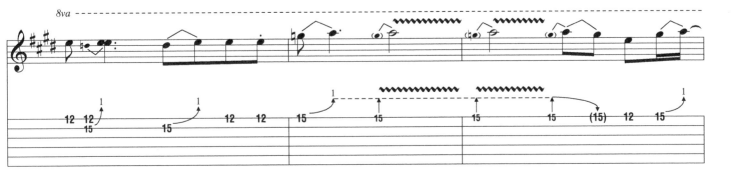

Cmaj7   D$_{add6}^{sus2}$

E5

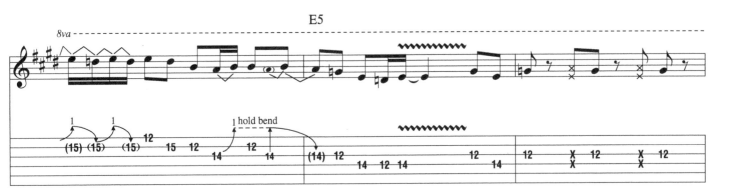

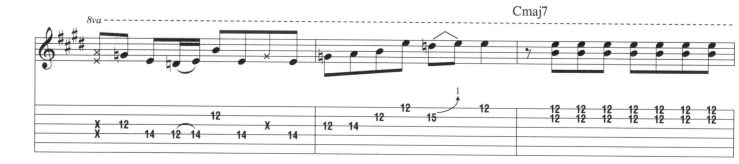

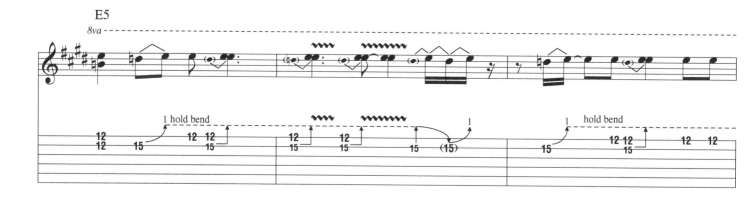

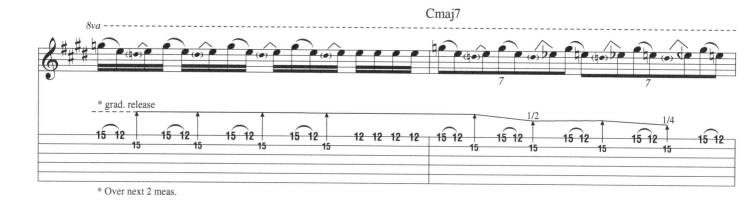

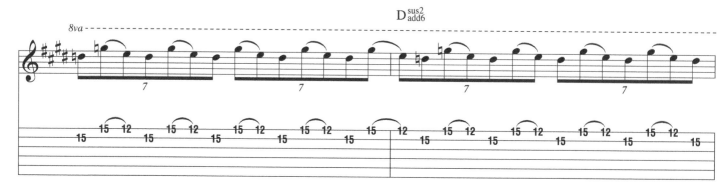

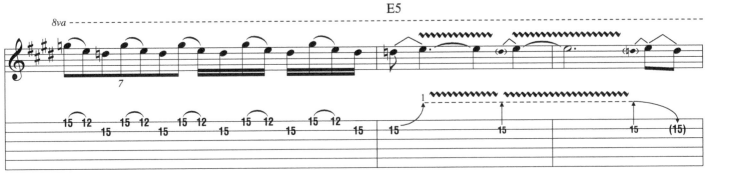

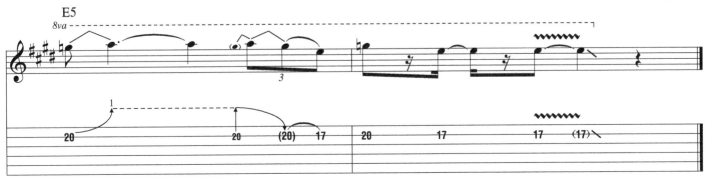

Additional Lyrics

2. I felt so good, like anything was possible.
   Hit cruise control, and rubbed my eyes.
   The last three days, and the rain was unstoppable.
   It was always cold, no sunshine.

3. I rolled on, the sky grew dark.
   I put the pedal down to make some time.
   There's somethin' good waitin' down this road.
   I'm pickin' up whatever's mine.

Into the Great Wide Open

Words and Music by Tom Petty and Jeff Lynne

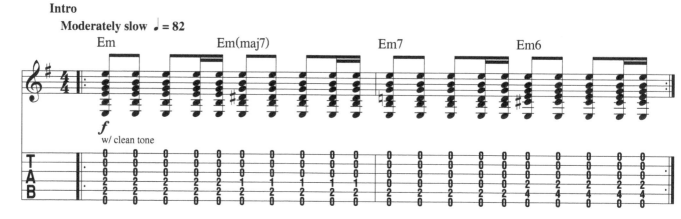

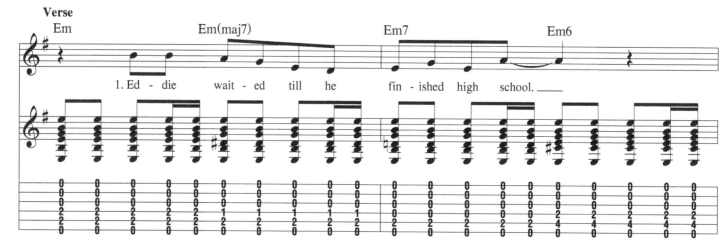

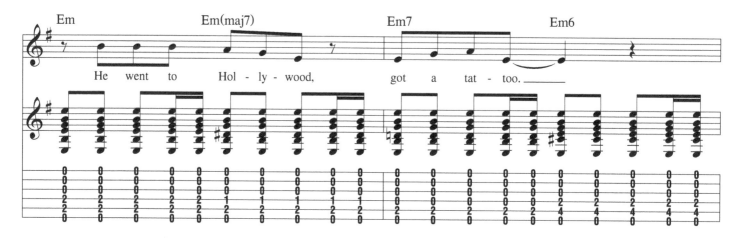

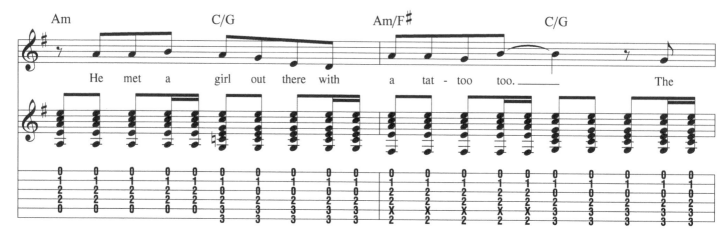

*T = Thumb on 6th string.

Chorus

In-to the great __ wide o-pen,

un-der them skies __ of blue. Out in the great __ wide

o-pen, a reb-el with-out __ a clue. __

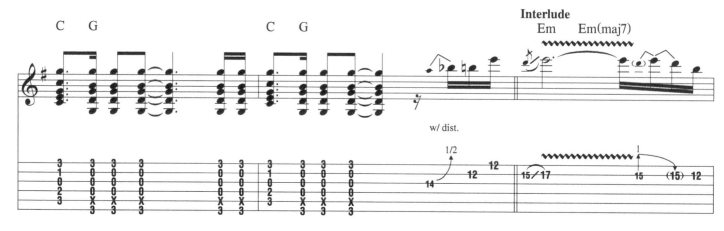

Interlude

w/ dist.

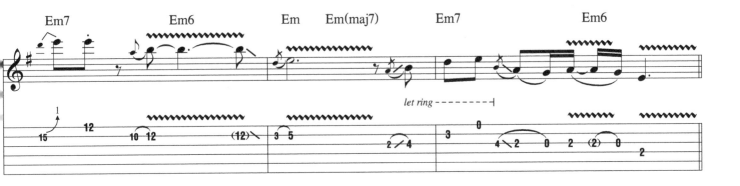

Verse

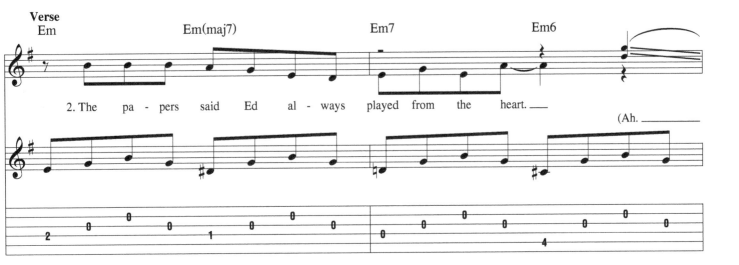

2. The pa - pers said Ed al - ways played from the heart. ___

(Ah. ___

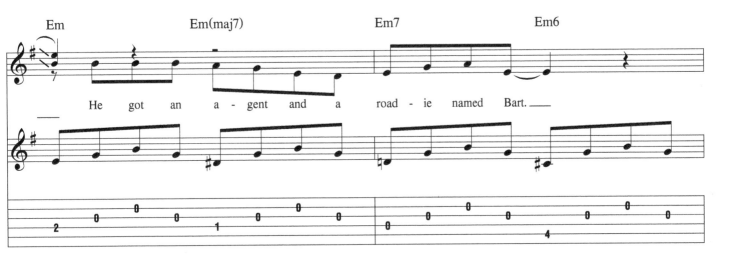

He got an a - gent and a road - ie named Bart. ___

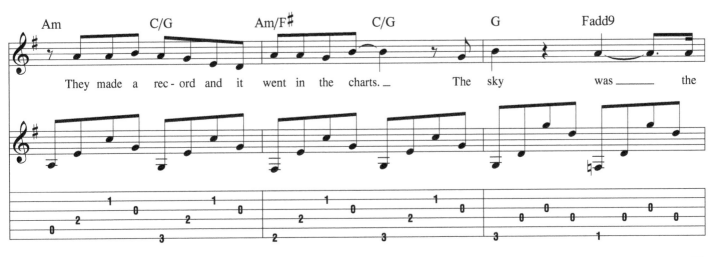

They made a rec - ord and it went in the charts. _ The sky was ___ the

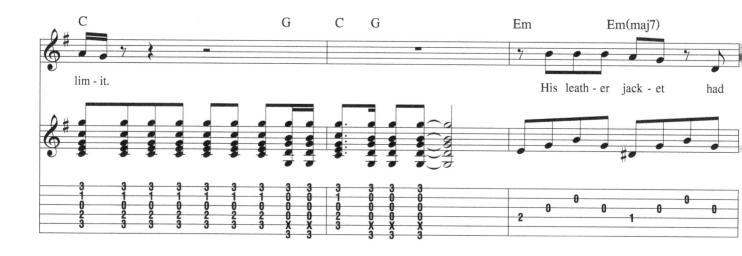

lim - it.

His leath - er jack - et had

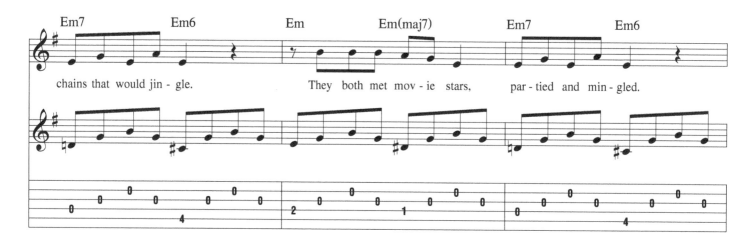

chains that would jin - gle.

They both met mov - ie stars,

par - tied and min - gled.

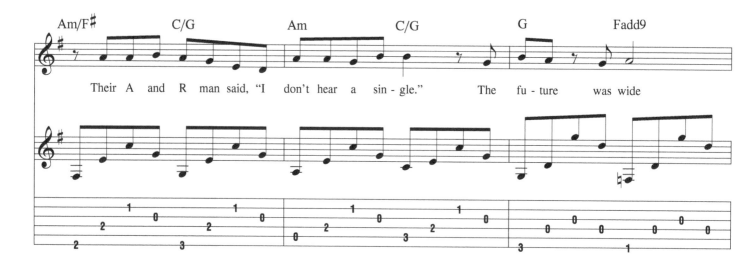

Their A and R man said, "I don't hear a sin - gle."

The fu - ture was wide

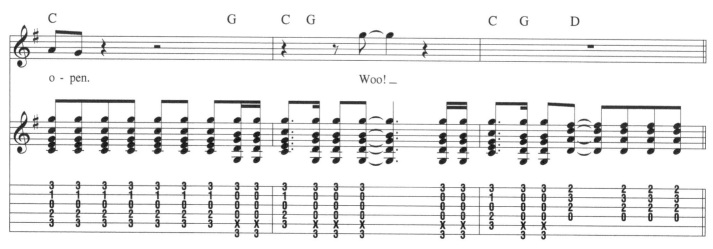

o - pen.

Woo! __

Outro-Chorus

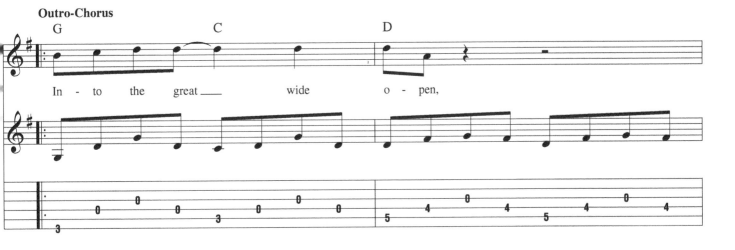

In - to the great _____ wide o - pen,

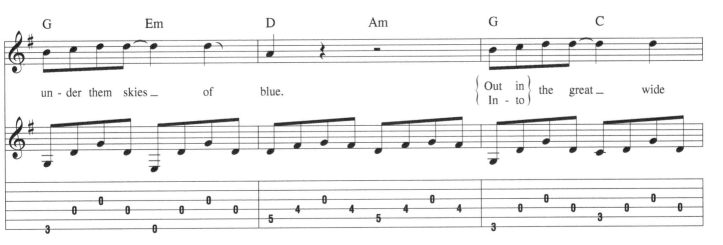

un - der them skies _____ of blue. { Out in / In - to } the great _____ wide

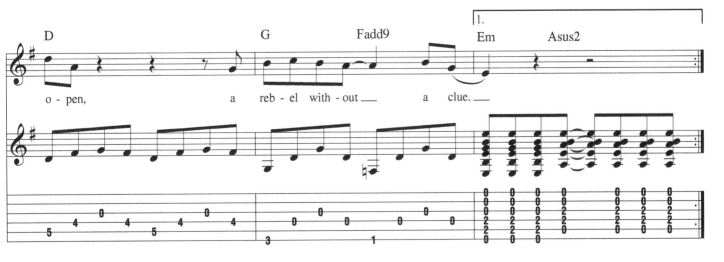

o - pen, a reb - el with - out _____ a clue. _____

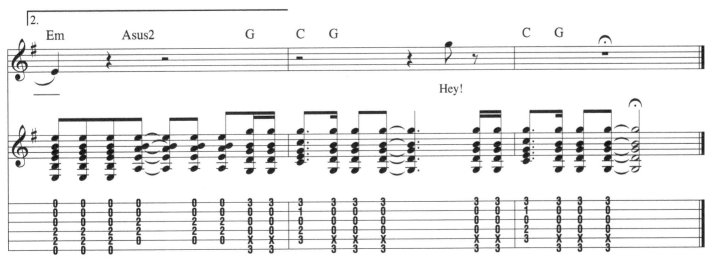

Hey!

Learning to Fly

Words and Music by Tom Petty and Jeff Lynne

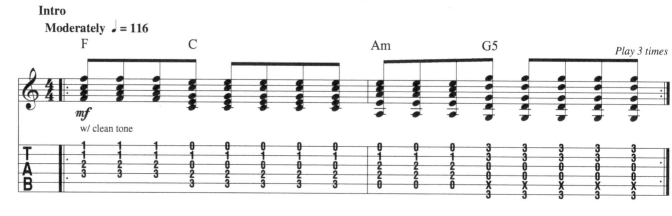

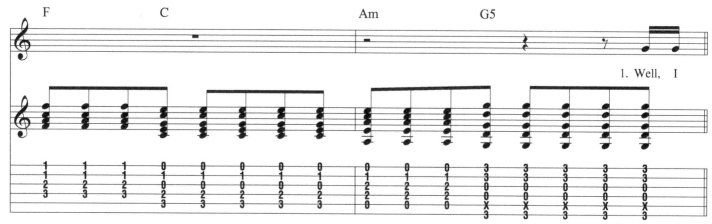

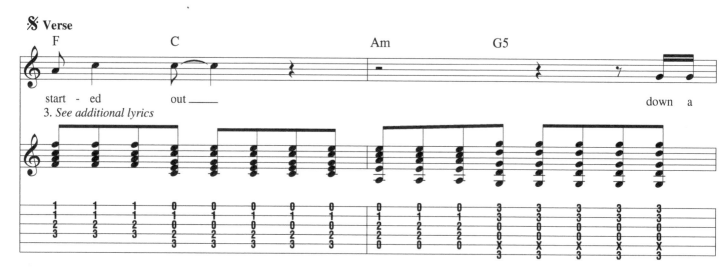

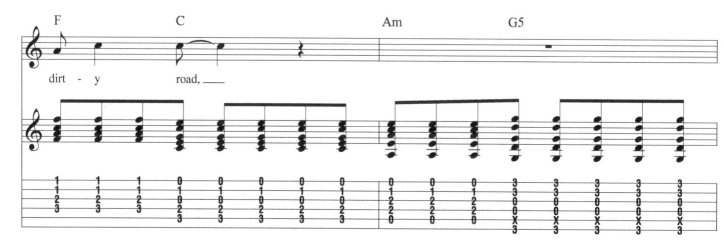

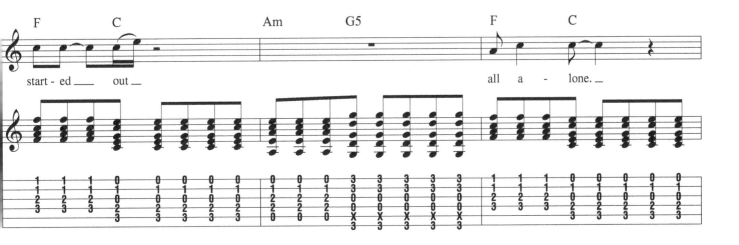

start - ed___ out ___ all a - lone. ___

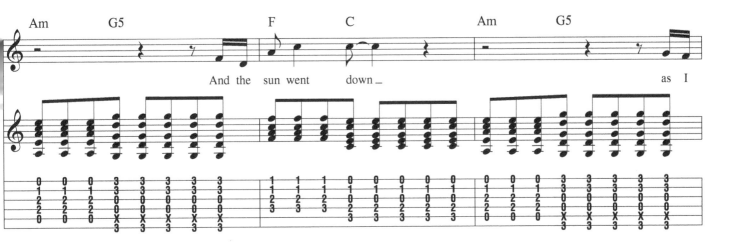

And the sun went down ___ as I

crossed the hill. ___ And the town lit up,

the world got still. ___ I'm

Chorus

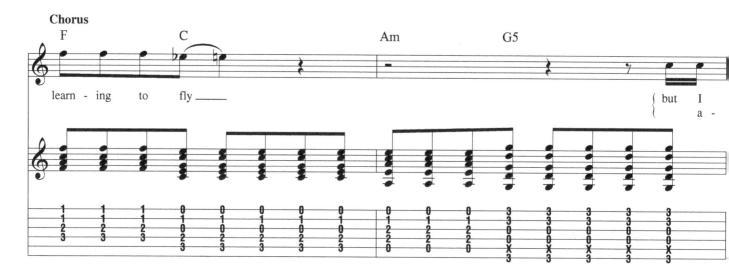

learn - ing to fly _____ { but I a -

ain't got   wings. _
round the   clouds. _

Com - ing _____ down _
What goes _____ up _____

To Coda ⊕

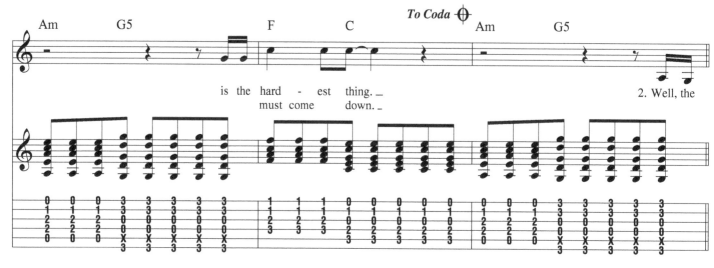

is the hard - est thing. _
must come down. _

2. Well, the

Verse

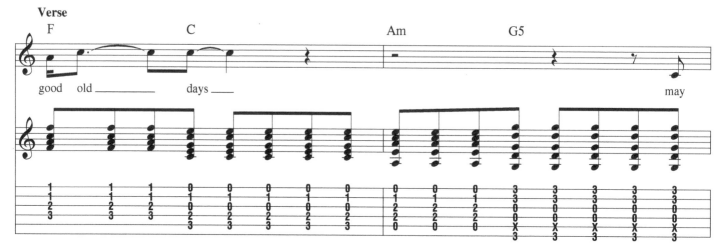

good old _____ days _____

may

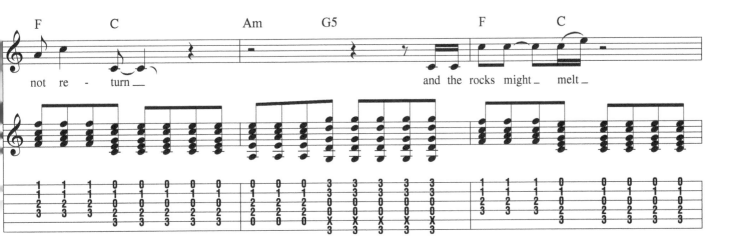

not re - turn ___ and the rocks might ___ melt ___

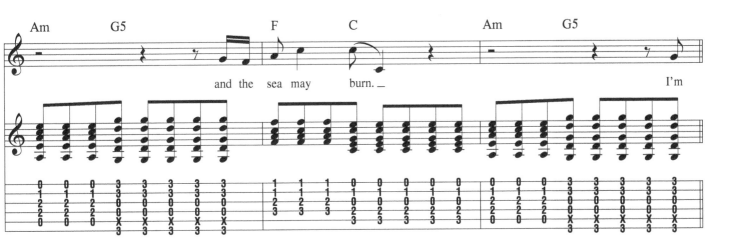

and the sea may burn. ___ I'm

Chorus

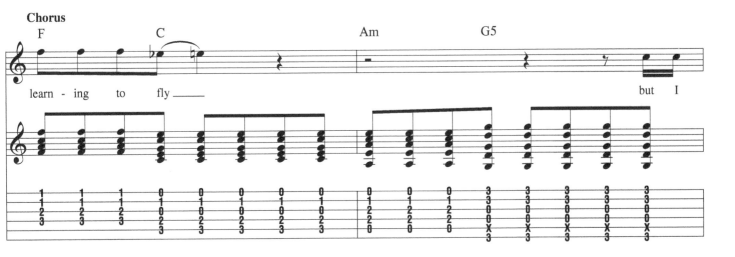

learn - ing to fly ___ but I

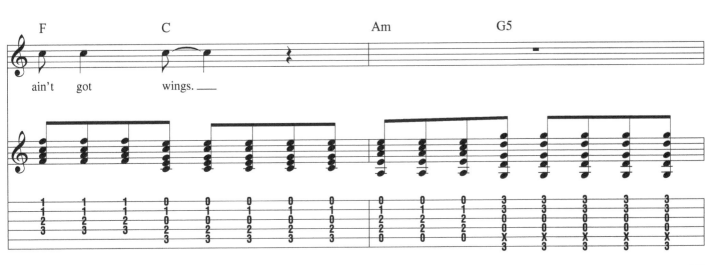

ain't got wings. ___

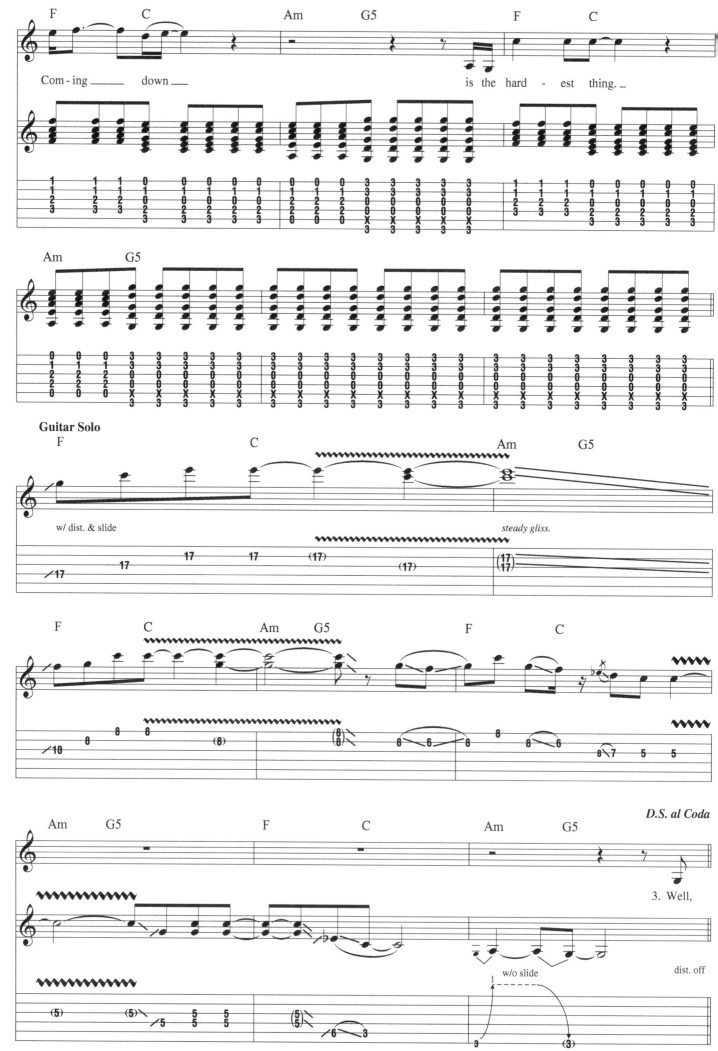

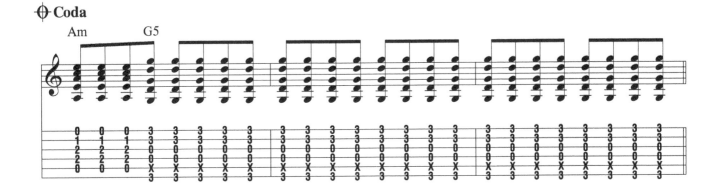

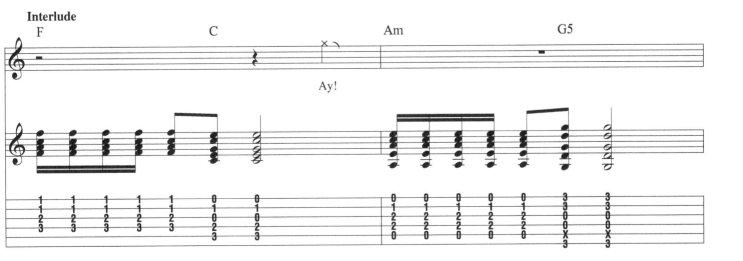

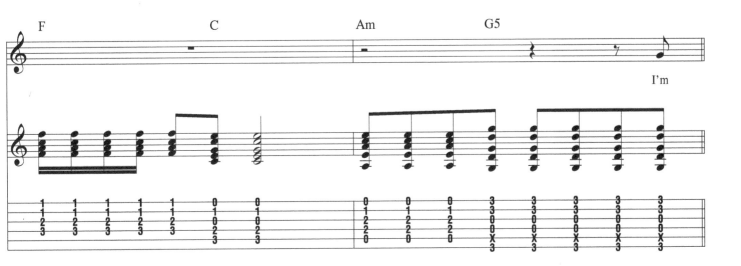

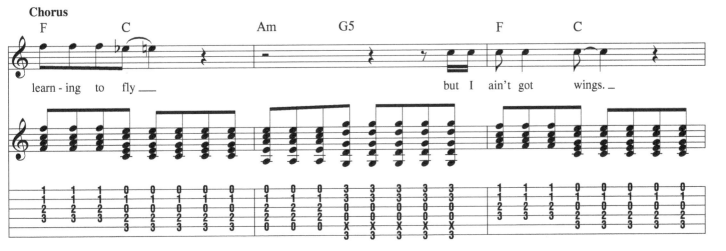

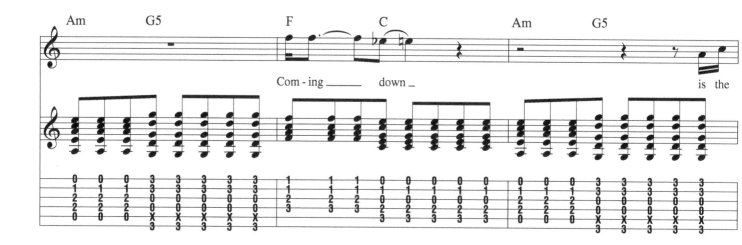

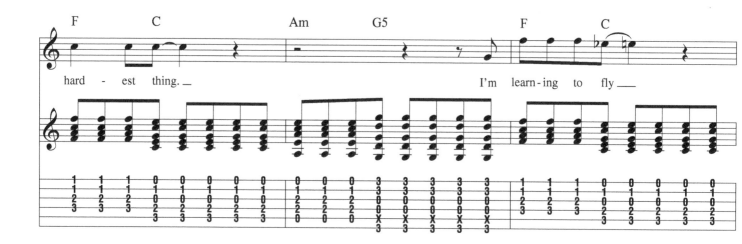

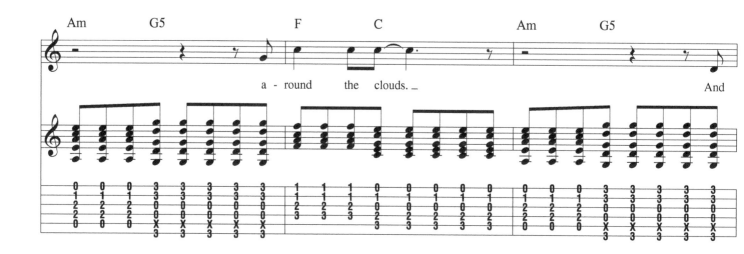

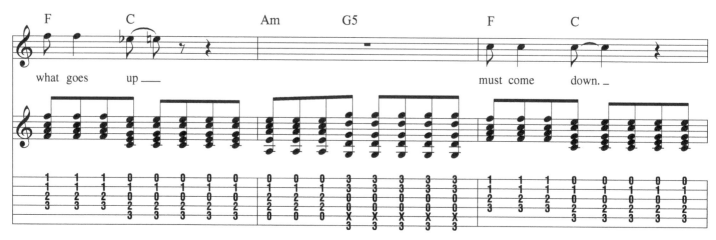

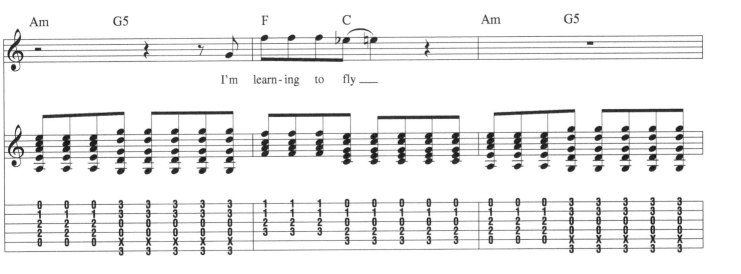

I'm learn-ing to fly ___

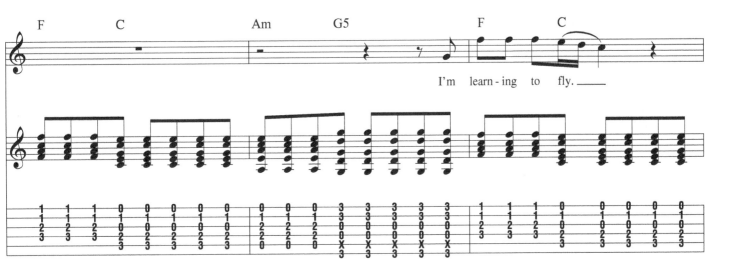

I'm learn-ing to fly. ___

Repeat and fade

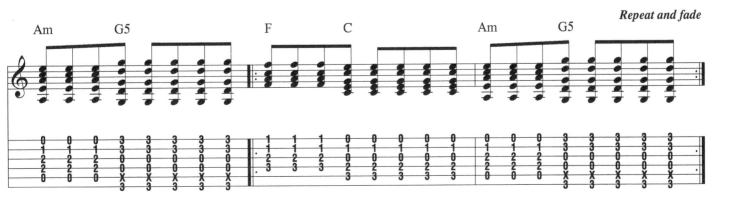

Additional Lyrics

3. Well, some say life will beat you down,
   And break your heart, steal your crown.
   So I've started out for God knows where.
   I guess I'll know when I get there.

Mary Jane's Last Dance

Words and Music by Tom Petty

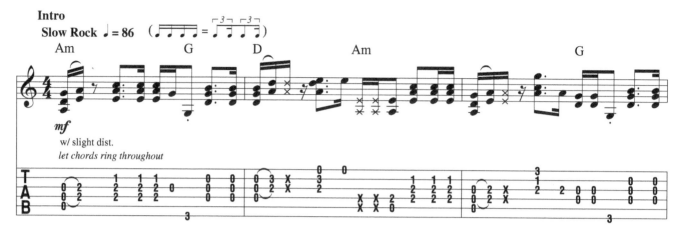

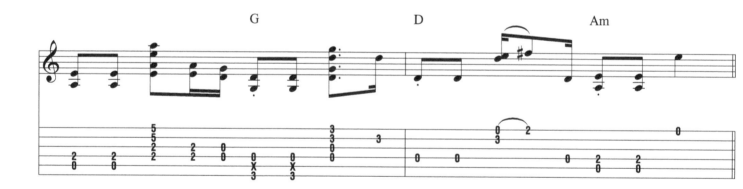

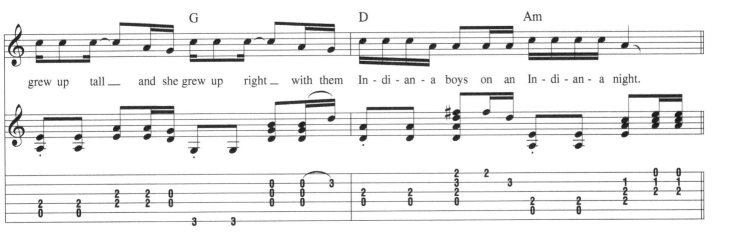

grew up tall __ and she grew up right __ with them In - di - an - a boys on an In - di - an - a night.

Interlude

(Hoo.) _____

Verse

(Hoo.) _____

2. Well, she moved down here at the age of eight - een, she

blew the boys a - way; was more __ than they'd seen. I _____ was in - tro - duced and we both start - ed groov - in', she

said I dig you, ba - by, but I got to keep mov - in' on. ___

Keep mov - in' on.

let ring - ⌐

Chorus

Last dance with Mar - y Jane, ___ one more time to kill ___ the pain. _____

I feel sum - mer creep - in' in ___ and I'm tired ___ of this town a - gain. ___

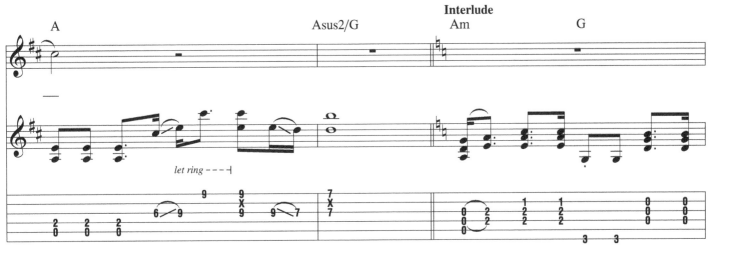

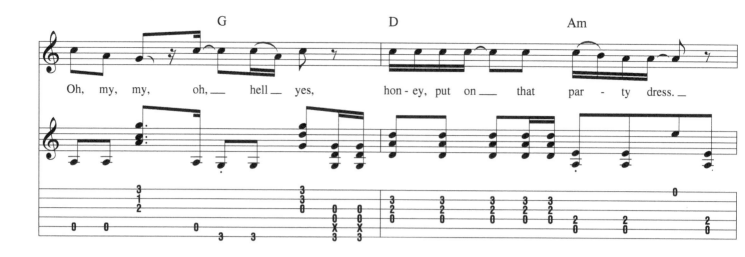

Oh, my, my, oh, hell yes, hon-ey, put on that par-ty dress.

Buy me a drink, sing me a song. Take me as I come 'cause I can't stay long.

Chorus

Last dance with Mar - y Jane, one more time to kill the pain.

To Coda

I feel sum-mer creep-in' in and I'm tired of this town a-gain.

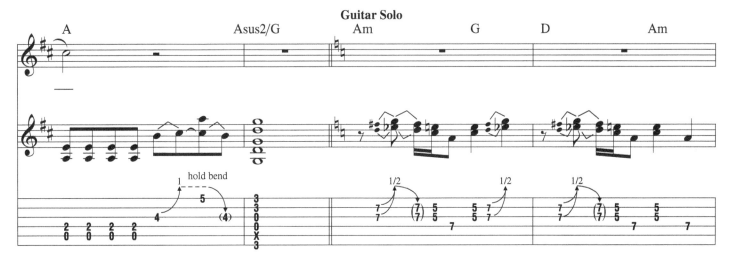

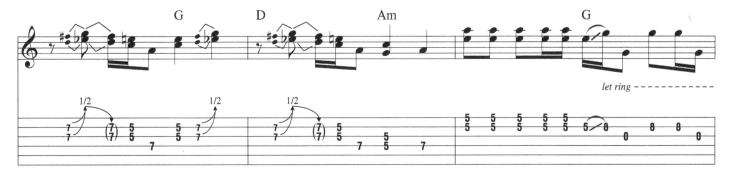

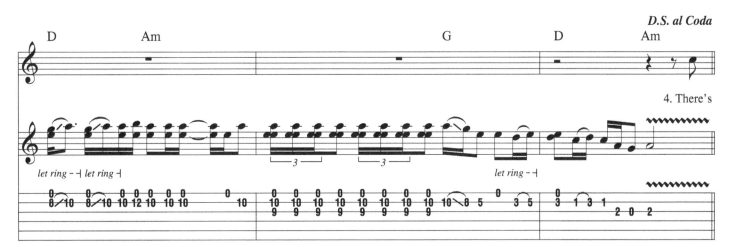

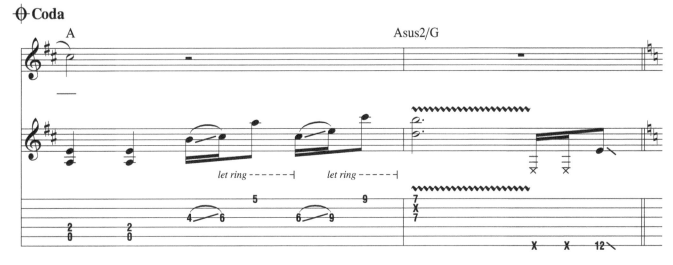

Interlude

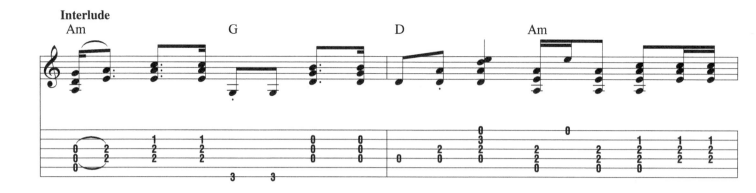

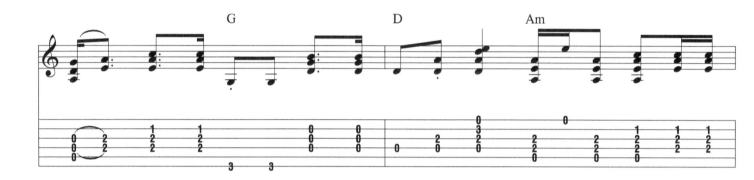

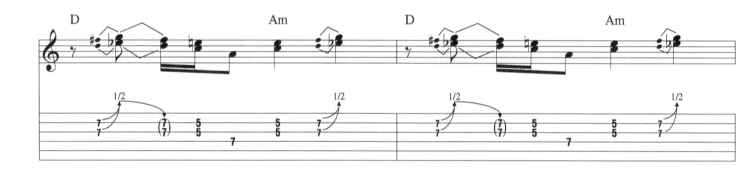

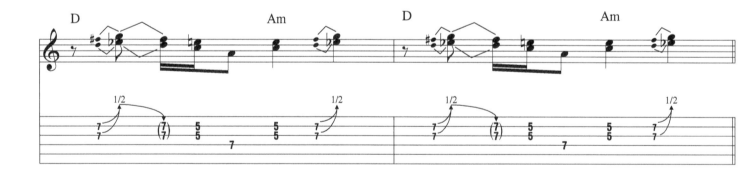

Outro-Guitar Solo

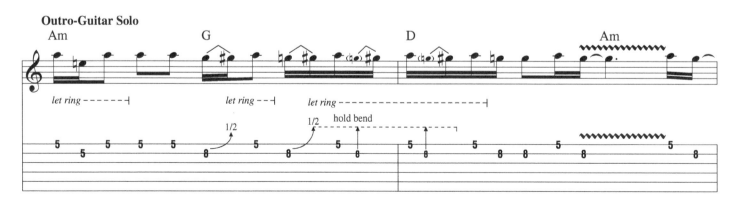

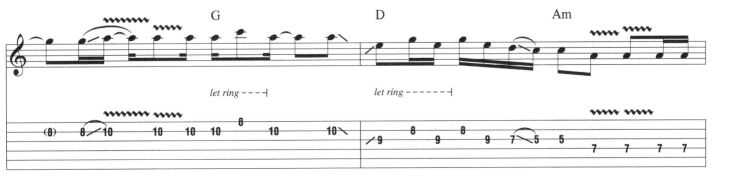

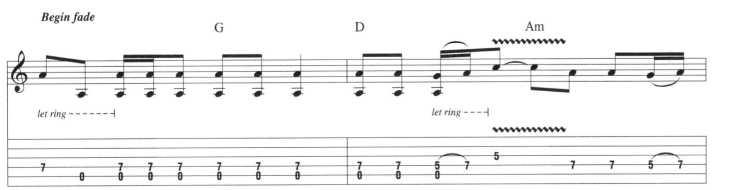

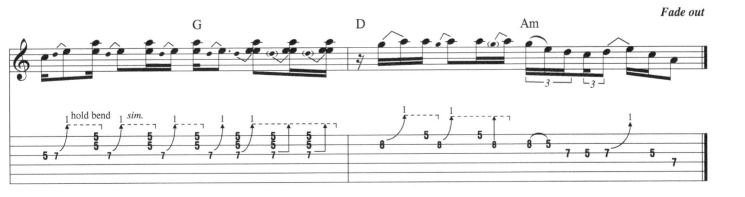

Additional Lyrics

4. There's pigeons down on Market Square.
   She's standing in her underwear,
   Lookin' down from a hotel room,
   And nightfall will be coming soon.
   Oh, my, my, oh, hell yes,
   You got to put on that party dress.
   It was too cold to cry when I woke up alone,
   Hit my last number, I walked to the road.

Refugee

Words and Music by Tom Petty and Mike Campbell

Intro

Moderate Rock ♩ = 116

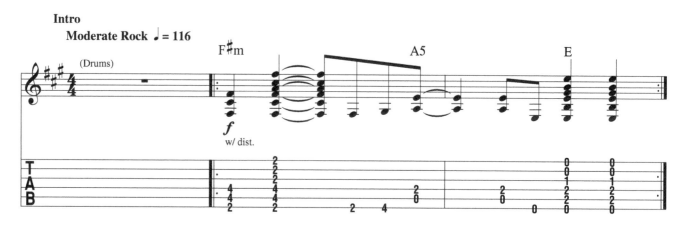

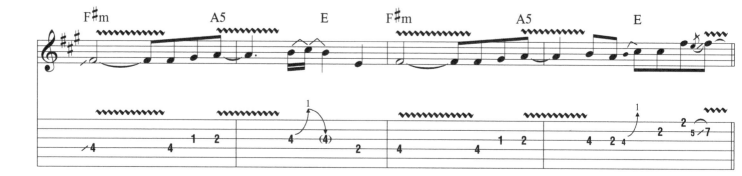

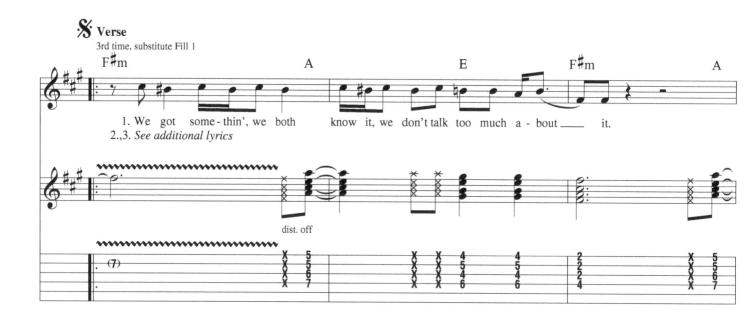

1. We got some-thin', we both know it, we don't talk too much a-bout _____ it.
2.,3. *See additional lyrics*

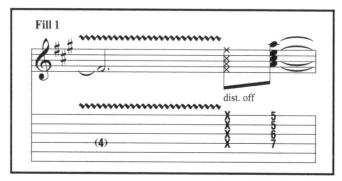

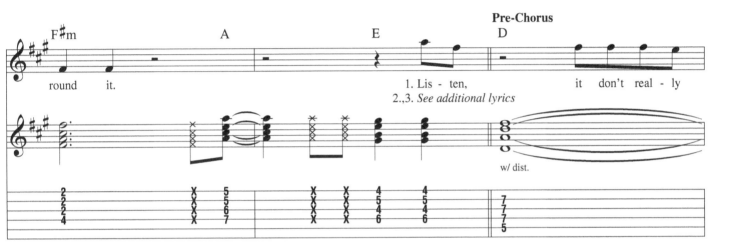

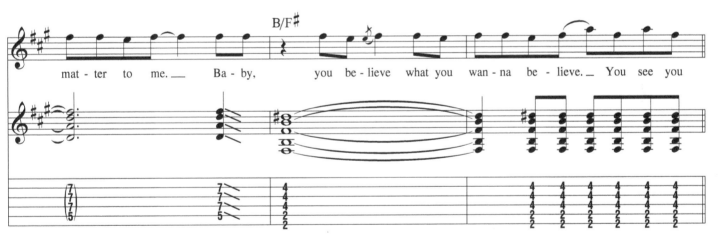

Now ba-by, you don't have__ to live like a ref - u - gee.__

(Don't have to live like a ref - u - gee.)__

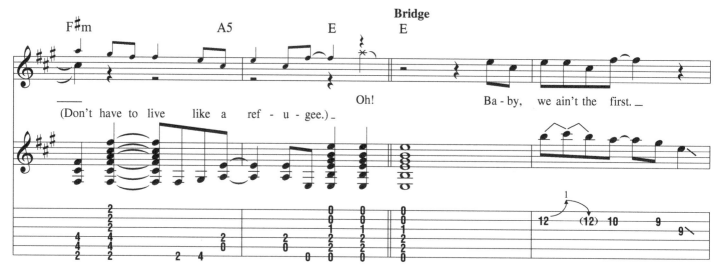

Bridge

(Don't have to live like a ref - u - gee.)__

Oh! Ba - by, we ain't the first.__

I'm sure a lot of oth - er lov - ers been burned.__

Right__ now this seems__ real

__ to you,__ but it's one of those things you got to feel to be true.__

Organic/Guitar Solo

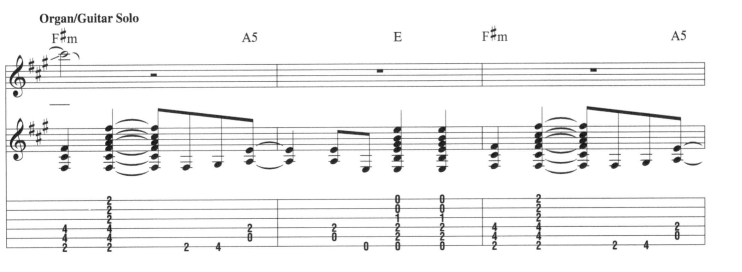

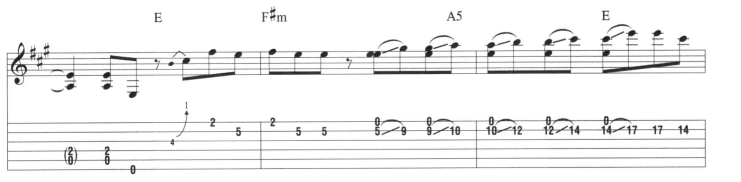

D.S. al Coda

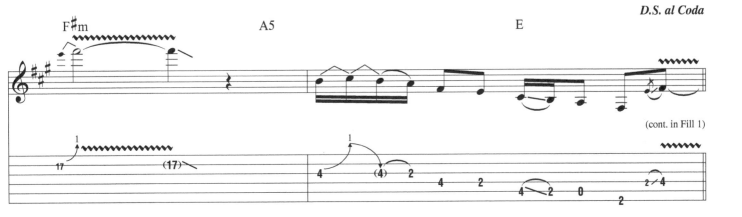

(cont. in Fill 1)

⊕ **Coda**

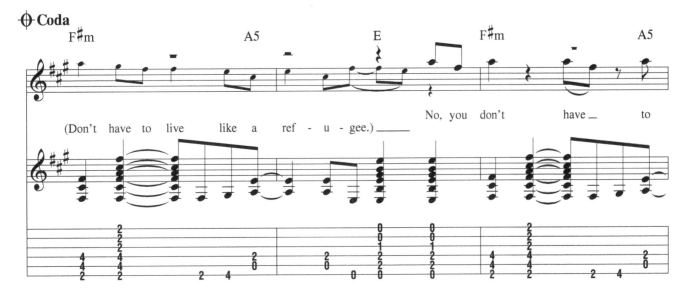

(Don't have to live like a ref - u - gee.) _____ No, you don't have _ to

live like a ref-u-gee. _____ Ba-by, you

(Don't have to live like a ref-u-gee.) _____

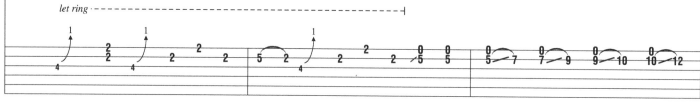

don't have __ to live like a ref-u-gee.

(Don't have to live like a

let ring -

Outro-Guitar Solo

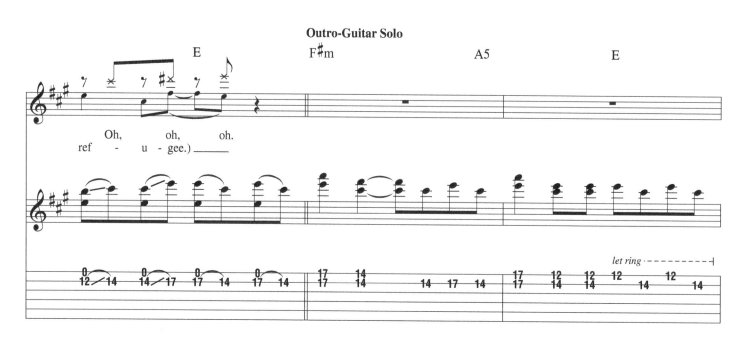

Oh, oh, oh.

ref - u - gee.) _____

let ring - - - - - - - -

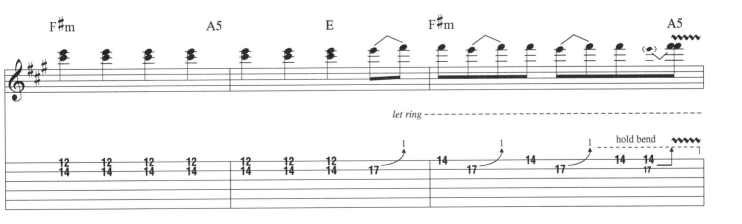

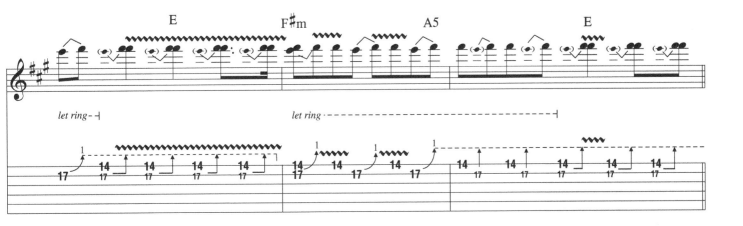

Repeat and fade

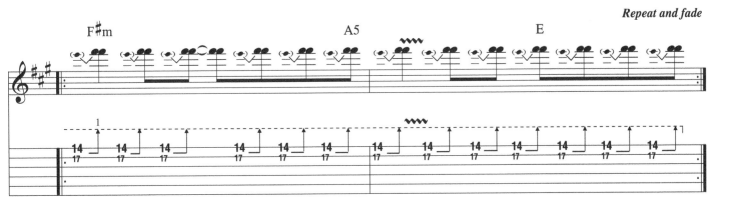

Additional Lyrics

2. Somewhere, somehow, somebody must have
   Kicked you around some.
   Tell me why you wanna lay there,
   Revel in your abandon.

Pre-Chorus 2. Honey, it don't make no diff'rence to me.
   Baby, ev'rybody's had to fight to be free.

3. Somewhere, somehow, somebody must have
   Kicked you around some.
   Who knows? Maybe you were kidnapped,
   Tied up, taken away and held for ransom.

Pre-Chorus 3. Honey, it don't really matter to me.
   Baby, ev'rybody's had to fight to be free.

You Don't Know How It Feels

Words and Music by Tom Petty

1. Let me run with you tonight, I'll take you on a moonlight ride.
2., 3. *See additional lyrics*

There's someone I used to see, but

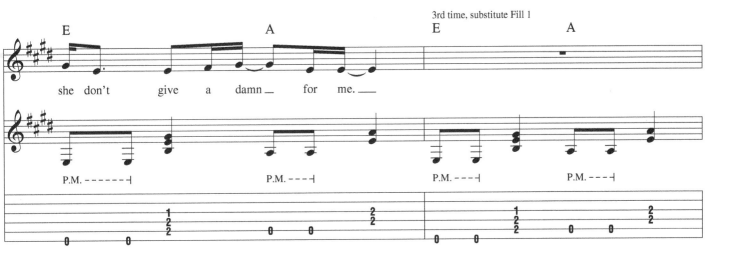

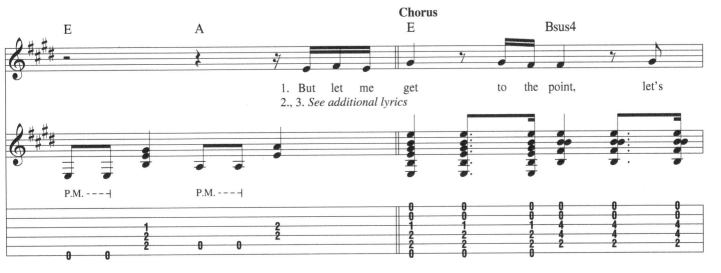

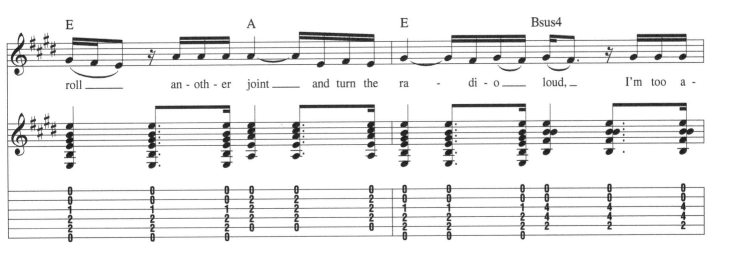

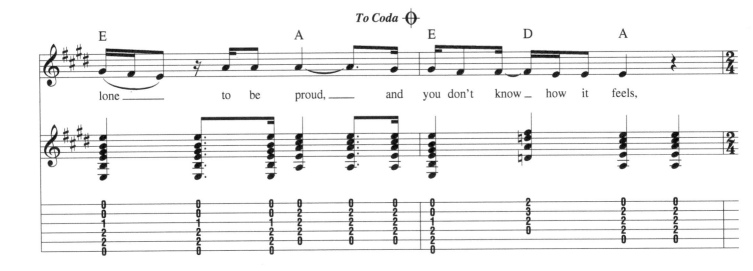

lone _____ to be proud, _____ and you don't know _ how it feels,

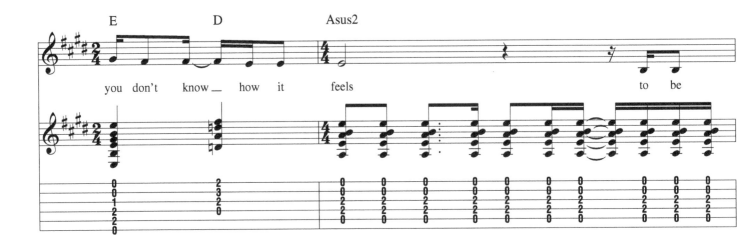

you don't know _ how it feels

to be

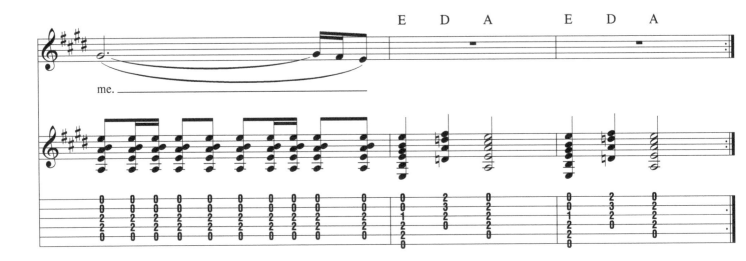

me. _____

Interlude

N.C.

Guitar Solo

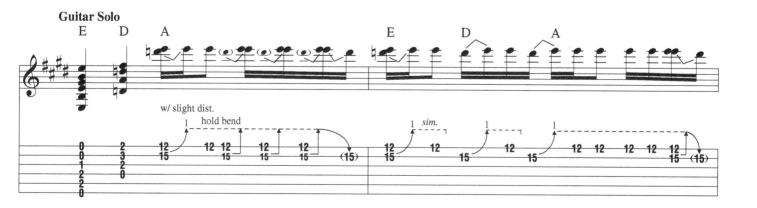

D.S. al Coda

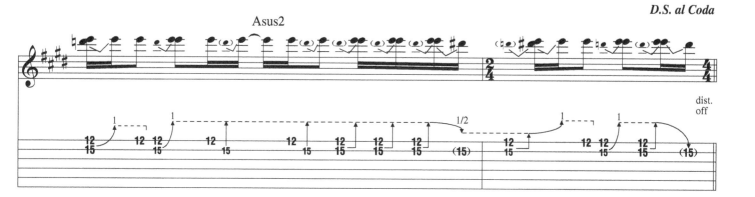

{ you / You } don't know_ how it feels, you don't know_ how it feels, no,

you don't know_ how it feels to be me.___

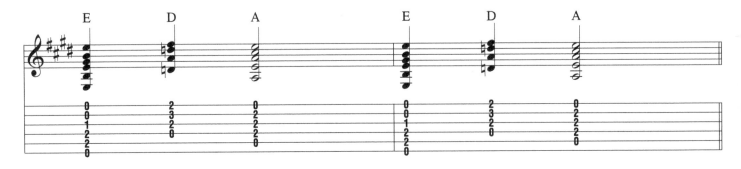

Guitar Solo

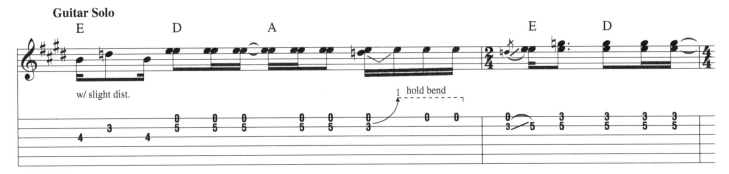

w/ slight dist.

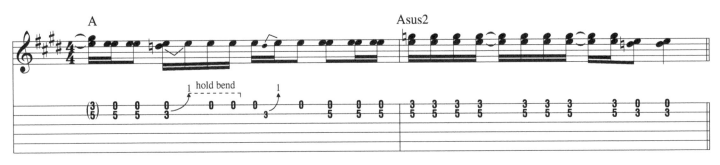

Outro

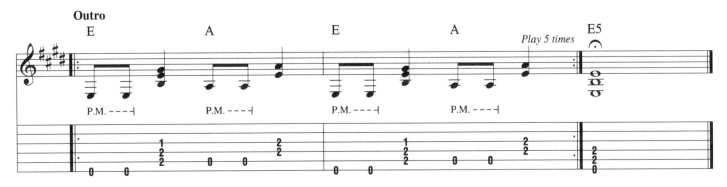

Additional Lyrics

2. People come, people go;
   Some grow young, some grow cold.
   I woke up in between
   A memory and a dream.

Chorus 2. So let's get to the point,
   Let's roll another joint
   And let's head on down the road to somewhere.
   I gotta go, and you don't know how it feels,
   You don't know how it feels to be me.

3. My old man was born to rock,
   He's still tryin' to beat the clock.
   Think of me what you will;
   I've got a little space to fill.

Chorus 3. So let's get to the point,
   Let's roll another joint
   And let's head on down the road to somewhere.
   I gotta go, and you don't know how it feels,
   You don't know how it feels,
   No, you don't know how it feels to be me.